THE PRIMARY TEACHER'S SCHOOL YEAR PLANNER

THE PRIMARY TEACHER'S SCHOOL YEAR PLANNER

Helping you focus on the things that matter

ELIZABETH HOLMES

CORWIN

Corwin
A SAGE company
2455 Teller Road
Thousand Oaks, California 91320
(0800)233-9936
www.corwin.com

SAGE Publications Ltd
1 Oliver's Yard
55 City Road
London EC1Y 1SP

SAGE Publications India Pvt Ltd
B 1/I 1 Mohan Cooperative Industrial Area
Mathura Road
New Delhi 110 044

SAGE Publications Asia-Pacific Pte Ltd
3 Church Street
#10-04 Samsung Hub
Singapore 049483

Editor: Amy Thornton
Senior project editor: Chris Marke
Cover design: Wendy Scott
Typeset by: C&M Digitals (P) Ltd, Chennai, India
Printed in the UK

Library of Congress Control Number: 2021936813

British Library Cataloguing in Publication Data

ISBN 978-1-5297-4227-5
ISBN 978-1-5297-4226-8 (pbk)

At SAGE we take sustainability seriously. Most of our products are printed in the UK using responsibly sourced papers and boards. When we print overseas we ensure sustainable papers are used as measured by the PREPS grading system. We undertake an annual audit to monitor our sustainability.

Contents

About the author

Elizabeth Holmes has had a long career in the world of education as a teacher, a writer, a teacher of teachers, a presenter, a learner, and a parent. After completing a degree in Politics and International Relations, she undertook a PGCE in Humanities and Social Sciences at the Institute of Education in London, where her love for learning was well and truly cemented!

While working in the education profession, Elizabeth also completed an MA in Creative Writing and Personal Development and a Postgraduate Diploma in Theology.

Elizabeth has written numerous books on education including A Practical Guide to Teacher Wellbeing (SAGE), as well as courses and conference presentations. She also writes articles on professional learning for Optimus Education and Eteach.com among many others.

Elizabeth has a special interest in helping teachers to thrive and really gain fulfilment in the education profession, and can be found championing teachers and learners on Twitter @EA_Holmes

About the contributor

Annelies Paris, also known by her online persona of Petite Primary, is a primary school teacher and YouTuber. She first developed an interest in teaching following her psychology bachelor's degree, which delved into child development and educational psychology.

Having qualified from her teacher training course and being awarded her QTS and PGCE in 2020, she has been supporting and empowering teachers through her YouTube channel. This channel started as a venture to document her own personal journey. However, it has since developed into a platform that provides advice and tips to support teachers in their journey, their confidence and their wellbeing. From activities such as offering recommendations on useful books and tools for training, to giving example answers to help nail a teacher training interview, Annelies has amassed over 2000 subscribers.

In line with her ethos about supporting the teaching community, she has also developed a hashtag #UnlockTeachTalk, which has teachers contributing from across the world. She is now a Year 1 teacher after spending a year teaching French to 650 pupils from Reception to Year 6. This has given her the experience to share her ideas and contribute to the themes found in this hugely beneficial planner for primary teachers.

About this year planner

Welcome to your Primary School Year Planner! It has been designed to support and inspire you throughout your year ahead, so you get as much fulfilment and enjoyment from your chosen career as possible.

Contributors to this planner have selected themes, reflections and activities to support your year, whether you are new to the teaching profession, in your early career development or an old hand wanting to view the coming year through fresh eyes.

As you travel through the year, you will notice subtle changes in your philosophy and practice of teaching. The experience you gain will feed into ever-developing professional confidence, which is likely to have an impact on your enjoyment of the job. Reflection is a powerful tool for teachers, too, so there are plenty of opportunities to jot down your thoughts in a way that will feed into your professional learning.

It is important to say that the information in this book is intended as guidance only and should not be taken as a replacement for qualified medical advice. If you find that you are struggling with the signs and symptoms of negative stress and anxiety, or any other symptoms that are troubling you, it is important to seek the advice of your GP, who will be able to signpost support.

This is your planner. Use it in the way that suits you and best supports you, and have a wonderful year ahead!

Add the dates
for the month

Monday	Tuesday	Wednesday	Thursday	Friday	Saturday	Sunday

Highlight/s

....

Notes

....

....

....

....

Checklist

☐

☐

☐

☐

One child, one teacher, one book, one pen can change the world.

Malala Yousafzai,

I Am Malala (2014)

September
- Key dates/Events:

 What, Where, Who ...

> **Date**

> **Date**

> **Date**

> **Date**

> **Date**

Whether you are a new teacher starting your first year in your first classroom or an experienced teacher with a sense of 'here we go again', September is a chance for a new beginning. A new class, perhaps a new classroom. Certainly, some new stationery supplies and blank sheets of paper!

Not all things need to be new and different though. There is no need to reinvent the wheel. If you have found a way of working that 'works' for you, stick with it. If you are still looking to refine your way of working – be inspired to try something new.

Use the space below to write down the new things you intend to try this year. Perhaps something you have learned about from a colleague, or gleaned from social media?

-

-

-

-

-

-

-

Professional Learning

The journey to thinking like a teacher

The process of 'thinking like a teacher' is not one that happens overnight. It requires reflection and effort and is something that tends to evolve over time. It is difficult to quantify, but it is something that feels 'normal' to those who practise it. If you are a new teacher, allow yourself time to get there.

Thompson and Wolstencroft list four key things that are useful to focus on when developing the professional skills required to 'think like a teacher':

1. *Begin to see yourself as a guide, not a teacher.* All of the children in your classroom have their own learning journeys. Your role is to guide them through their own learning, not to simply fill them with knowledge.

2. *Remember that you are one of the most consistent role models the children in your class will see.* Your approach to things will influence how the children view them. It is not only important to be enthusiastic about what you are teaching, you also need to be confident in children's abilities to achieve.

3. *Recognise when things need to change. Go 'off piste' and deviate from your plans.* Thinking like a teacher means that you learn to embrace the possibility that things might not work out. What do you have to lose by changing your approach?

4. *Develop a positive and resilient attitude. Children won't always be positive.* They will act in a way that you won't have predicted. You need to rise above it all, model a positive approach and ensure that you display the resilience that a teacher needs.

(Thompson and Wolstencroft (2021))

Classroom Ideas

What matters in your classroom?

Consider the values of your school and your personal teaching ethos and how you will demonstrate these in your classroom.

☐ Want to encourage reading for pleasure? Set up an appealing reading corner that welcomes children and encourages them to try out new authors or genres.

☐ Are you passionate and knowledgeable about the positive impact of mindfulness and emotional regulation in children? Set up a calm corner where children can have stimuli to help them regulate their feelings or breathing exercises to allow them to self-regulate.

Preparing all of this early allows you to introduce these themes from the get-go and means you can reinforce them throughout the year. These are just two examples. It can be anything from having particular books on a theme (such as diversity, inclusion, mindfulness, equality), to allocating a display to your personal values.

The CLPE's core books list is a great place to start if you want to get some new books for your classroom:

https://clpe.org.uk/corebooks

Corebooks helps primary schools choose the very best children's books for their school or classroom libraries. This site contains a comprehensive selection of high-quality books for children from ages three to eleven and a selection of free teaching plans.

What themes and values do you want to highlight? How will you do this? Use this space to make plans for your classroom.

Notes:

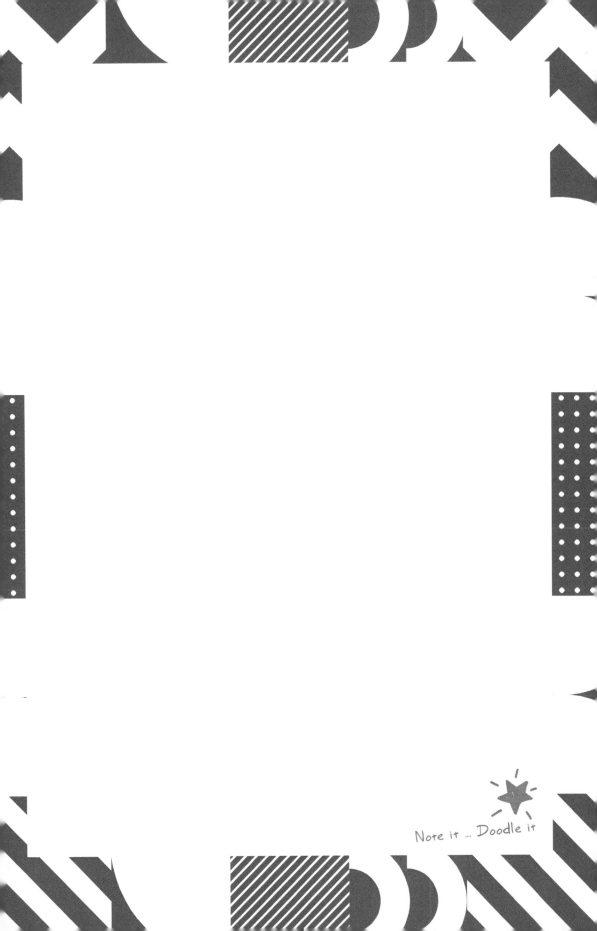

Note it ... Doodle it

Wellbeing Toolkit

Start as you mean to go on

The beginning of a new year is a great time to focus on developing sound wellbeing habits that will last. It might be that you have done this before but that your good intentions did not last long once pressures started to build. This doesn't matter. Begin again.

☐ Accept that your wellbeing matters, and always has

☐ Know that small changes to our daily lives and routines can make a real and lasting difference to our wellbeing

☐ Know that you will not always get the balance right but that keeping wellbeing in mind as a goal *will* make a difference

When it comes to wellbeing, we all need to be in it for the long haul. Gimmicks, short cuts and top tips will come and go, but the importance of focusing time and thought on what gives us a sense of wellbeing is a constant.

☐ Teaching is an incredible profession to be a part of. Let's help ourselves, and each other, to thrive.

Use the space here to jot down some small changes that you aim to make. It could be spending time for yourself every week doing something you enjoy. It could be ensuring that you block out time during the week that will be work-free.

You may not always be able to achieve this but if you write it down here, you might be more likely to remember to concentrate on it.

Make time for/to: _____

Monday	Tuesday	Wednesday	Thursday	Friday	Saturday	Sunday

OCTOBER

Highlight/s

....

Notes   **Checklist**

.... ☐

.... ☐

.... ☐

.... ☐

Education should not be a predetermined journey with a map already drawn, with no ability to leave the path or pause. It should be a co-adventure.

Greg Bottrill,

School and the Magic of Children (2020)

October
- Key dates/Events:

 What, Where, Who ...

Date

Date

Date

Date

Date

Learning can be an adventure for teachers and children. Throughout the school year you will learn together – albeit different things. Knowing your class is perhaps the most important starting point for this adventure.

Across the world, children in primary education spend an average of 799 hours in the classroom each year (source: OECD, 2020). This is a lot of time together!

Use the space below to jot down some ways in which you can find out more about your class as individuals or a group. Have a think about how this knowledge may be useful to influence your teaching and the time you spend together.

-

-

-

-

-

-

Professional Learning

Every child in your class

One thing that we need to remember as teachers is that although we teach *classes*, those classes contain *individuals* with myriad needs, likes, dislikes and aptitudes that may shift and change as the year progresses. It is so important to get to know each child as an individual as much as possible. These ideas may help:

1. ***Communication –*** Talk to the SENDCO to make sure you have all the information you need about children with SEND and any other children who have come to the SENDCO's attention. It is important to ask for help if you are unsure how to best meet these needs.

2. ***Knowledge –*** Make sure you know the relevant child development milestones for the year group you are teaching. There is a useful guide here: https://inourplace.co.uk/developmental-and-emotional-milestones-leaflet/
   Knowing where the average child will be in his or her physical and emotional development at any age and stage can help to ensure that expectations are age appropriate. Remember that these milestones can only ever be guidelines.

3. ***Self-regulation –*** Self-regulation strategies can be really useful in the classroom and you can find out more about the research supporting them here: https://educationendowmentfoundation.org.uk/evidence-summaries/early-years-toolkit/self-regulation-strategies/

4. ***Cohesion –*** While it is important to know each child in their own right, it is also important to notice how they relate to each other as a group. What brings them together? What encourages cohesion? What helps the day to flow easily? Noticing these things can help build a sense of community in your classroom, and to develop that notion of co-adventure.

Classroom Ideas

Getting to know you . . .

Building relationships with pupils should be your priority from the start of the year. Positive relationships should be actively maintained throughout the whole academic year. Naturally, this can be done in many different ways, be it in the small moments that you spend talking with an individual child or in the time spent creating whole-class activities to promote good teamwork skills and rectify tensions amongst peers.

Some ideas:

☐ Ask children to introduce each other so that they listen carefully to their peers

☐ *What would you rather?* Cut the classroom in two with an invisible line. Ask children what they would prefer between two options. Children must go to whichever side they prefer. These can be as sensible or as silly as you like!

☐ Get the children to create fact files or 'top trumps' about themselves

☐ Q&A in small groups and to the teacher

☐ Miming game: guess a fact about the child (best for older years)

☐ Colour tests for fun: what does your favourite colour/choice of colour from a selection of options say about you?

Jot down some ideas that might work for you and your class . . .

Notes:

....

....

....

....

....

....

....

....

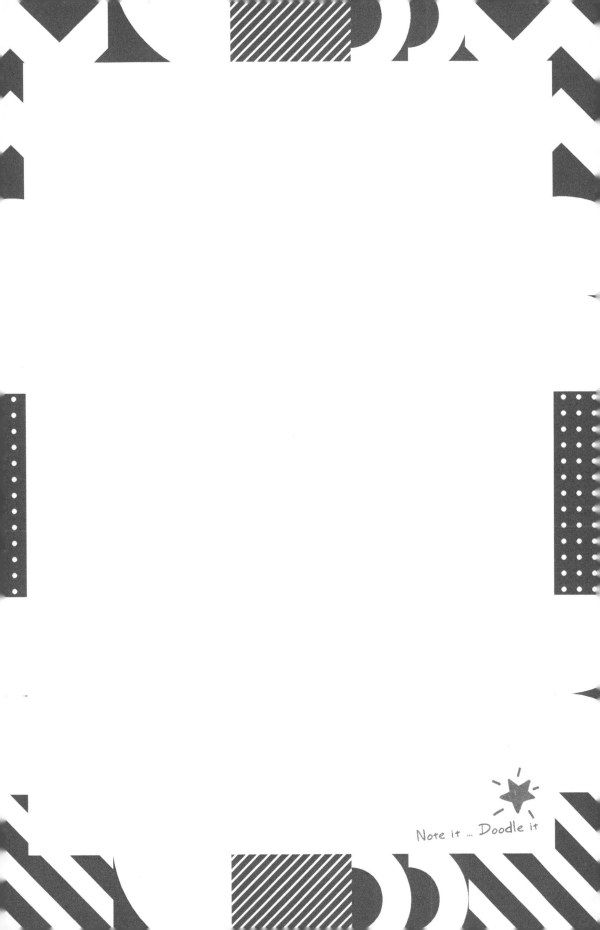

Note it ... Doodle it

Wellbeing Toolkit

What works for you?

Self-knowledge is crucial when it comes to safeguarding your sense of wellbeing. While some people love spending time with others to replenish their wellbeing, others need time in solitude. While some need to be active to boost feel-good feelings, others gain more from rest and relaxation. We are all different, which is why one size does not fit all when it comes to creating balance in our lives.

These ideas may help you to think about what wellbeing means for you:

1. *Remember what helps* – Write down what you know helps you to feel an enhanced sense of wellbeing. It can be anything, big or small. For example, your best chocolate treat or your best place to visit on holiday? Your favourite country walk or the meal you most look forward to? A friend you love spending time with or your favourite tipple? Write down whatever gives you a sense of being nurtured and of addressing balance in your life. Keep your list somewhere you will see it regularly to remind you! You may want to make a wellbeing board with photos or pictures as a visual reminder.

2. *Make a commitment* – Even though the term is in full swing and time is short, commit to doing at least one thing per day from your wellbeing list or board. Remember, even small gestures can have a positive impact on your wellbeing.

3. *Develop an attitude of gratitude* – Writing down three things that you are grateful for at the end of each day has been shown to have a positive impact on your overall wellbeing. Keep a gratitude journal beside your bed and read back over it every now and then.

Jot down what helps and a few thoughts on what you can be grateful for.

Make time for/ to: _____

Add the dates for the month

Monday	Tuesday	Wednesday	Thursday	Friday	Saturday	Sunday

NOVEMBER

Highlight/s

....

Notes

....

....

....

....

Checklist

☐

☐

☐

☐

I have learned that the best way to lift one's self up is to help someone else.

Booker T. Washington,

Story of My Life and Work (1900)

November
- Key dates/Events:

What,
Where,
Who ...

Date

Date

Date

Date

Date

Working with parents is not always easy or fun. It is, however, always important. Evidence from the EEF toolkit estimates that effective parental engagements can make a difference of up to 3 months in learning gains over the school year (EEF, 2018).

Remember that many parents find communicating with teachers difficult too. They may have had bad experiences of school. They may not have the confidence to raise issues with you.

It is useful to approach parents' evening with an idea of what you want to achieve. Do you want to ask any specific questions about any children? What messages do you want to get across to the parents that you speak to? Jot some thoughts down here.

-

-

-

-

-

-

-

Professional Learning

Teamwork can make the difference

Teamwork can make the difference between loving and hating your job. If you feel isolated at work, it could be because the team structures in your school are not strong enough to provide the support you need.

Remember, even if teamwork is not a strong point in your school, you can build networks with other teachers in a similar position to you in your locality or via social media. Twitter has many teacher members. You are bound to find someone doing a similar job to you to share ideas with.

These ideas might help:

1. *Give and take* – Be aware of your strengths so you can support others with tasks you can do well. If you have development needs, ask for support from a colleague.

2. *Be generous with ideas* – If you can see an easier way of achieving a task, offer your suggestions.

3. *Watch and learn* – Take every opportunity to learn from colleagues through informal chats. Find out more about how others work in your school. Ask colleagues questions about how to improve areas of your work you are struggling with. This helps to develop openness – a foundation of great teamwork.

4. *Check in with others* – A great way of helping to boost your own wellbeing is by supporting others. Checking in with colleagues, asking how they are, and getting to know what makes them tick can go a long way towards building cohesion in your school.

Classroom Ideas

Meeting parents

Whether you are an NQT or an experienced teacher, the approaching date of parents' evening might fill you with dread. Be prepared, not just for the information you will share with parents, but also to ensure you are physically and mentally ready for a potentially long evening or two.

Here are some tips about how to help the evening to go as smoothly as possible:

☐ Make sure you have a bottle of water or hot drink to keep you going. There's nothing worse than having a sore throat in a situation where you're expected to do most of the talking! Some generous schools provide snacks for staff to keep energy levels up. If they aren't provided, have plenty of your own to keep you going!

☐ Stick to the appointed times you allocated so that the parents waiting don't get frustrated and you don't have to stay any longer than you have to.

☐ Have a script/results/work in front of you that you plan to talk about. What have you recently covered? How did they do in a specific assessment? Mention strengths and areas to improve on. Any questions?

☐ Make sure you have an easy meal ready for when you get home. You probably won't feel like cooking from scratch after a long day!

Are you ready? Use this space to plan what you need to do.

Notes:

....

....

....

....

....

....

....

....

....

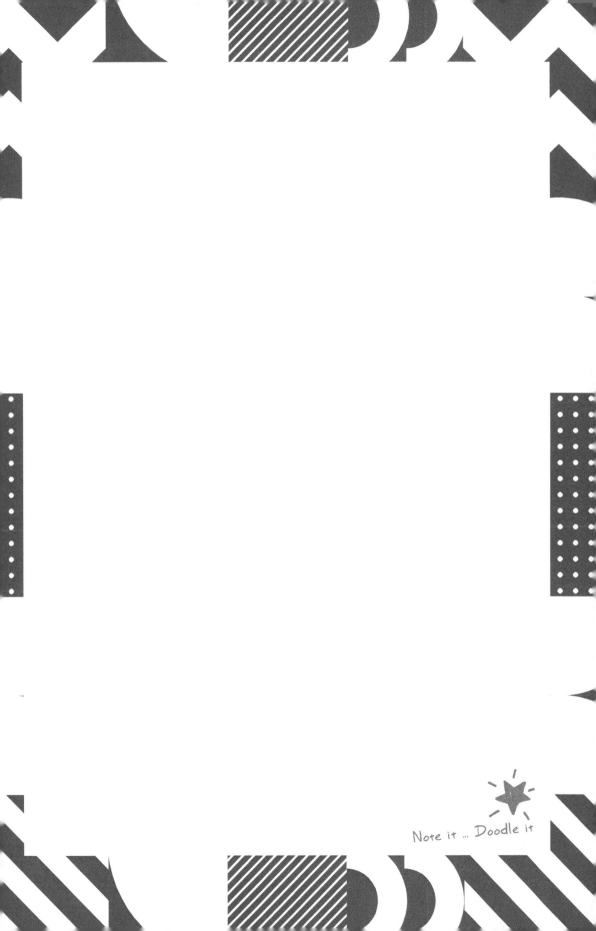

Note it ... Doodle it

Wellbeing Toolkit

Making connections

When life gets busy and work seems to take up all your spare time it is easy to feel swamped and to lose touch with friends and family. You might even find yourself withdrawing from colleagues at school as you attempt to get through your 'to do' list. Yet connecting with others is one of the main ways in which we can boost our wellbeing. It is important to reach out when we can.

These ideas may inspire:

1. *Make time* – Schedule time to meet up with friends, whether in person or via the internet or phone. It is so easy not to do this if you don't set time aside.

2. *Reach out* – Is there someone you know who is struggling? Get in touch to share your experiences and boost each other.

3. *Listen well* – It is easy to slip into the habit of listening superficially when we are swamped with work. But that does nothing to enhance connection with others. If at all possible, really listen when you are having a conversation with someone else. Aim not to multi-task so that the other person has your full attention. This can transform the quality of your communication and your connection with others.

4. *Belong* – We all have a need to belong. The social connection we get from a sense of belonging can do wonders for our overall wellbeing. Often, working in a school offers myriad opportunities to develop that sense of belonging, but if you still don't feel that, seek out opportunities for other ways to belong in your wider community, maybe through interest groups, sports, politics or hobbies.

How will you prioritise making connections with others for your wellbeing? Make some notes.

Make time for/to: _____

Add the dates for the month

Monday	Tuesday	Wednesday	Thursday	Friday	Saturday	Sunday

Highlight/s

....

Notes

....

....

....

....

Checklist

☐

☐

☐

☐

Find the good. It's all around you. Find it, showcase it and you'll start believing in it.

Jesse Owens,

Blackthink (1970)

December
- Key dates/Events:

What,
Where,
Who ...

Date

Date

Date

Date

Date

This month will be extra busy for many teachers. School performances, Christmas parties and Christmas lunches are all a change from the 'normal' routines of the school, which can bring great fun and joy. But this break from the norm can throw up all kinds of challenges. Some children find it hard to cope with changes in routine, others may not feel a part of the excitement.

December is often the month where children get to perform on stage and 'do' drama. The value of drama and performance for learning is much discussed and researched. The CLPE's popular *Power of Reading* programme surveyed teachers using the programme and 88% of them said that the use of drama in the teaching sequences was the most beneficial of the teaching approaches used (CLPE, 2018).

Use the space here to consider your own views about the importance of drama. Has it been important in your life and learning? It is an effective part of your teaching?

-

-

-

-

-

Professional Learning

Mantle of the Expert

Given the potential benefits to be gained from high-quality drama in schools, it is worth considering ways of making more use of it in your teaching. *Mantle of the Expert* is an approach to drama that uses fictional contexts in which children take on the role of an expert team. They work on the carefully planned challenge which involves tasks and activities that will see them exploring areas right across the curriculum. For example, a class of children may play the role of archaeologists excavating an Egyptian tomb, or they might be documentary makers, or publishers – the possibilities are endless.

The key elements of Mantle of the Expert include:

☐   The children are given expert roles

☐   They set up a fictional enterprise (they know that what they are doing is not real — the children consciously go into and come out of the fiction)

☐   They are set tasks by the 'client' (the teacher) and these tasks will usually involve a range of curriculum areas

☐   They work collectively through imagination, problem solving and inquiry

What children learn when inside the fiction can lead into curriculum learning outside the fiction.

If you would like to find out more about Mantle of the Expert or do the free online introductory course visit www.mantleoftheexpert.com

Classroom Ideas

Hot seating

This month you may be busy with a Christmas performance, but drama is not just for Christmas! Drama can open up learning for children in surprising ways. This idea can be used across any subject where it fits.

The term '**hot seating**' describes exactly what the activity is. Someone is put into the *hot seat*, in role, and other children in the group ask questions, often to find out the motivation of the characters in the hot seat. The role is usually a fictional character but can be a character from history or an official who has to answer questions from journalists or concerned villagers, for example. It is important that all the children are given a role (such as that of a journalist) so that they are fully involved. You as the teacher should be prepared, at least initially, to be the one in the hot seat. Some suggestions:

☐ Goldilocks and the three bears are each being 'interviewed' about their thoughts on the events in the story.

☐ A famous historical character you are studying (perhaps Rosa Parks?) could be interviewed about her refusal to move seats on a bus when asked.

☐ You could use the activity to get the children to think about different views about school uniform, or gendered sports.

☐ You could use it to explore the subject of bullying and to encourage children to think about the thoughts and feelings of others.

How could you use this learning activity with your class? Make some notes about what might work for you and your teaching.

Notes:

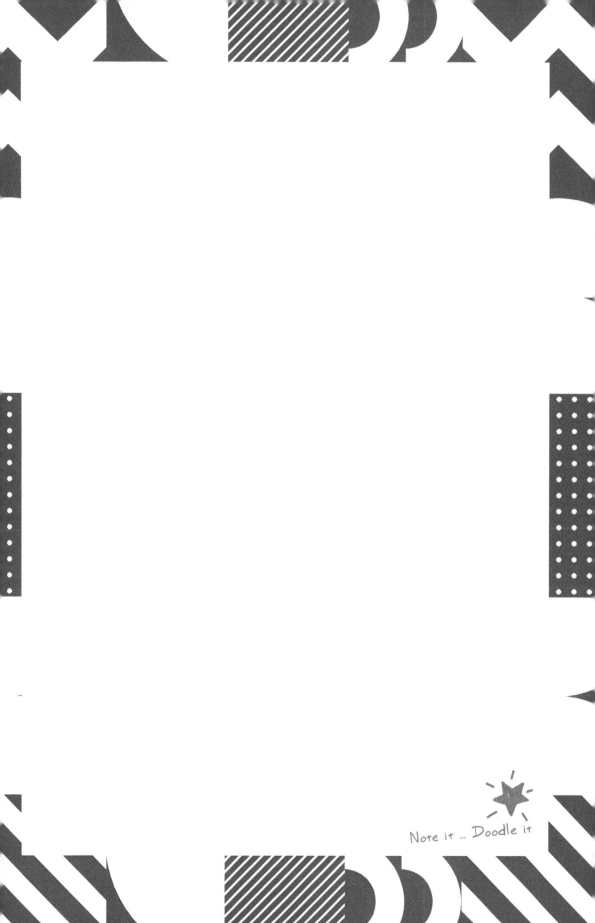

Note it ... Doodle it

Wellbeing Toolkit
Busy times

You may find that you are busier than ever this month. While that may not normally be a problem, this is also a dark month that comes at the end of a very long and full term. And on top of the extra demands at school, your homelife may become busier too if you are organising festivities and have your own children at school.

Take a deep breath. Busy does not necessarily mean stressful so hopefully there is plenty of enjoyment to be had from these weeks before the end of term. These ideas may help:

☐ *Pace, pace, pace* — When you know you are going to be extra busy it is important to pace yourself. Even if you are really enjoying the extra activity, your body and mind will need down time. Schedule in some breaks and treats and don't let anything else get in the way of them! These don't have to be grand gestures. Anything that helps you to feel refreshed and nurtured will help.

☐ *Say no!* — There will be some things, the end of term festivities for example, that cannot be postponed, but other tasks can be. Say yes to what has to be done and no to what can be delayed. This will help to keep your workload on an even keel.

☐ *Plan for when the 'busy' is over* — It is not uncommon for teachers to crash when the high pressure is over. Just keep in mind that you may be more vulnerable to catching a virus or having a flare up of old symptoms when you are exhausted, so plan some less demanding days as soon as you can so you give yourself a chance to recover. Eating well and remembering to take in enough fluids is important, and you may want to take some nutritional supplements as well.

Whatever is the cause of your busy-ness this December, aim to enjoy it as much as you can!

Make some wellbeing plans. When can you see that the demands will be easing? What small gesture to yourself will help you to feel nurtured?

Make time for/to: _____

Add the dates for the month

Monday	Tuesday	Wednesday	Thursday	Friday	Saturday	Sunday

JANUARY

Highlight/s

....

Notes

....

....

....

....

Checklist

☐

☐

☐

☐

Our glorious diversity – our diversities of faiths and colours and creeds – that is not a threat to who we are, it makes us who we are.

Michelle Obama,

Speech at the White House (2017)

January

- Key dates/Events:

 What, Where, Who ...

Date

Date

Date

Date

Date

We should celebrate the glorious diversity of our classrooms not just because inclusion matters but also because there is so *much* to celebrate! In recent years, more and more classroom resources have been published that can help you to bring diverse voices into your teaching, so it is easier than ever before to be more inclusive.

Being an inclusive teacher, who runs an inclusive classroom, is all about understanding the ways in which communities can operate to the benefit of some and the detriment of others. It is also about fully understanding that cultural diversity is a huge strength in a classroom.

Committing to celebrating diversity is one strong step towards declaring your classroom a space in which everyone can thrive – and that is the greatest gift we can give to our students.

What will you do to celebrate diversity in your classroom? Make some plans . . .

-

-

-

-

-

-

Professional Learning
Diversity and you

Diversity is. It exists and it contributes tremendously to the overall quality of our life experiences. Diverse and multicultural communities need to promote inclusion and equality of opportunity to ensure that everyone can thrive and achieve their best.

Making sure that children learn about difference in a positive way is so important if we are to have cohesive communities. Helping them to understand that regardless of race, gender, age, religion, disability or sexual orientation, everyone is of equal value and must be treated equally and fairly is absolutely key.

If you want to make your classroom more inclusive, these top tips will help:

1. Challenge every negative attitude you hear in your classroom

2. Be totally committed to treating everyone fairly and equally

3. Make sure everyone in your classroom knows exactly what your rules are for how you treat one another. Follow up on every transgression

4. When planning lessons, make sure they reflect the diversity in your room, community, region and country. Take a global perspective where possible

5. Assess the resources you use for diversity. Would each child in your classroom be able to see themselves reflected in the resources you use?

6. Have a read of your school's policies through an inclusion and diversity lens. Can you suggest any changes?

7. Be really hot on challenging stereotypes, and make sure you don't let any slip into your examples or resources

8. Think about the ways in which children participate in your lessons. Does anyone face a block that you can help to remove?

Classroom Ideas

Do you really know how diverse your class it?

It is likely that you know a lot about the children in your class by now. You will especially know those children classed as EAL. Children with English as an Additional Language do not always struggle with English learning. Bilingual children (and even multilingual children) can be high achievers in all language learning. There may be children in your class who can speak a language other than English that you do not know about. There may be children with family members of different nationalities that you are unaware of. A good activity to help these children share their identities is to ask the class –

☐   *What languages do you speak at home?*

☐   *What languages do people in your family speak?*

This can be a whole class discussion or in smaller groups.

This could lead to children sharing knowledge and experiences of different cultures with their peers in smaller groups. It might be that children are willing to share phrases and words that are part of their language experiences.

Perhaps there are children in your class with more to share – if only they were asked?

This is just one way to find out about the diversity of your class. What other ways could you do this? How can you encourage the children in your class to share their experiences of cultural diversity?

Notes:

....

....

....

....

....

....

....

....

....

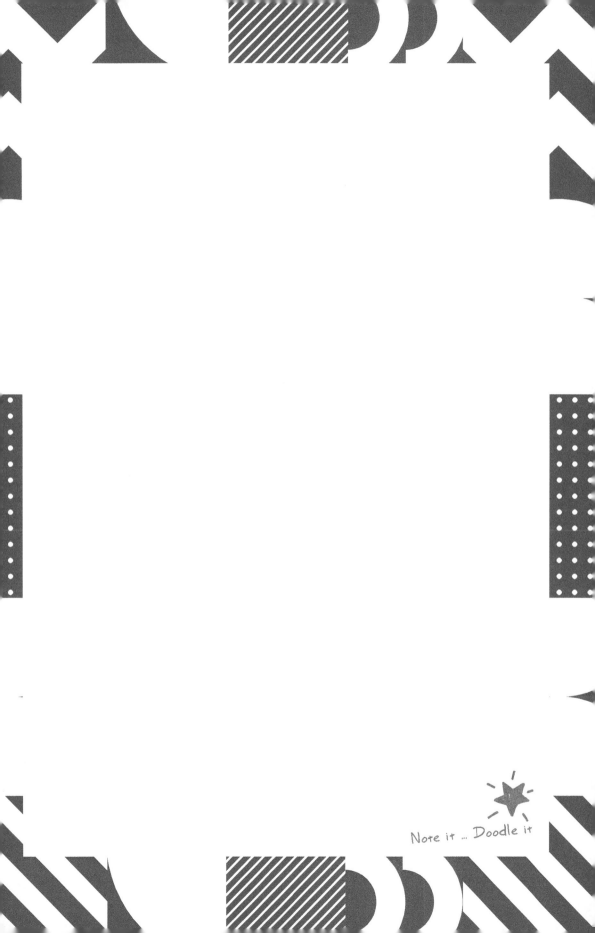

Note it ... Doodle it

Wellbeing Toolkit

Sleep the good sleep

There is no doubt that sleep is a cornerstone of wellbeing, and good quality sleep is the holy grail of feeling good and being fit for the day ahead.

By contrast, sleeplessness is debilitating. It drags us down and makes getting through each day a slog. We cannot function at our best and it is more likely to make us feel that life has no joy. So it is really important to get as much great quality sleep as we possibly can, regardless of how busy we are.

These tried and trusted tips may help:

☐ Aim for a regular bedtime each night. This will help to get your body into the habit of sleep at a certain time.

☐ Wind down your 'busy-ness' as you approach bedtime. Give yourself some pure relaxation time.

☐ Avoid watching or listening to the news last thing at night, or getting involved in debates on social media. Aim for something more relaxing and that won't wind you up or leave you feeling angry or frustrated.

☐ Keep your bedroom as clutter-free as possible. A calm relaxing space is bound to help you to fall asleep.

☐ If sleep evades you, talk to your GP. If there is a particular issue that is preventing you from sleeping, aim to deal with it — there will be help out there for you.

Use this space to keep a brief sleep diary to help you to determine what works for you when it comes to getting a great night of sleep. Log the time you went to bed, what you ate, how you spent the half hour before you went to bed, any dreams you had and what time you woke up. Can you spot any patterns?

Make time for/to: _____

Add the dates
for the month

Monday	Tuesday	Wednesday	Thursday	Friday	Saturday	Sunday

Highlight/s

....

Notes

....

....

....

....

Checklist

☐

☐

☐

☐

I have not failed.
I've just found
10,000 ways
that won't work.

Thomas A. Edison,

How to Succeed as an
Inventor (1882)

February
- Key dates/Events:

What, Where, Who ...

Date

Date

Date

Date

Date

February can be a difficult month. Grey days can turn into grey weeks. It can be hard to stay positive. 'Wet play' is rarely something that children or teachers relish. It is a good time to remind yourself that failure is a fabulous learning tool. Children should not be afraid of mistakes. They are an important part of learning.

This goes for teaching too. Disastrous lessons are valuable things. Not only do they show you what doesn't work, they also show that failures are nothing to shy away from. The teacher taking stock during a lesson, acknowledging that it is not working and changing plans models for children that this is OK. Things don't always go to plan. What matters is accepting that it has gone wrong, being OK that this has happened and 'bouncing back'.

Have a think about times in the past when a failure has taught you something. Make some notes . . .

-
-
-
-
-
-

Professional Learning

Powerful encouragement

There are many debates in the world of education, but one thing we can all agree on is the importance of being relentlessly encouraging. When children are not at the level we think they could be working at the word 'yet' is a powerful motivator. We cannot predict the future but we can be entirely optimistic about how much our pupils can achieve.

Think about encounters you have had in the classroom. Can you think of any times where children have lost motivation? What contributed to that? What got them back on track? These points may help your reflections:

1. Notice how frequently you use the word 'yet' when talking to children. It can be a powerful motivator.

2. Be specific when praising a child's work. For example, 'your use of adjectives in your writing is really improving!'

3. Focus on developing intrinsic motivation in children – reliance on external praise is not a sustainable form of motivation.

4. Use encouragement words as liberally as possible and focus on the process of their work.

5. Encourage resilience in the face of perceived failure. Acknowledge effort and be specific about what elements of the strategy used to complete the task were successful.

6. Help children to plan for future success. What needs to change and what can remain the same?

You may be interested in positive psychoogy and its use in schools. There is plenty of information online, or you could explore the theme more in *Psychology for Teachers* (2021) by Paul Castle and Scott Buckler.

Classroom Ideas

The power of yet

Arguably one of the most important words in education is the word 'yet'. Children often label themselves as being 'good' or 'bad', at a subject or a skill very early on. As a form of encouragement for children, using the word 'yet', can send out a message of hope and motivation, and create ambition. Just picture the following scenario:

Child 1: 'That was the easiest one so far, give us a harder one.'

Child 2: 'I don't get it; I can't do it.'

Teacher: 'You will get there! Don't forget, everyone learns at different speeds. It's not a race. Try saying 'I don't get it …yet.' You will understand soon, do not worry.'

The teacher is not invalidating the child's feelings but is encouraging them to keep persevering. The teacher is also sending a message to the other children in the class who might have already passed certain stages, to be mindful of others and that we all have the ability to succeed.

For more inspiration search the internet for 'The power of YET'.

How can you harness the power of yet in your classroom? How can you show children that some things take longer to learn than others? Can you help them to plot their learning of something specific on a graph? They can then look back at how the learning happened. Would this work for a particular unit you are teaching? Make some notes . . .

Notes:

....

....

....

....

....

....

....

....

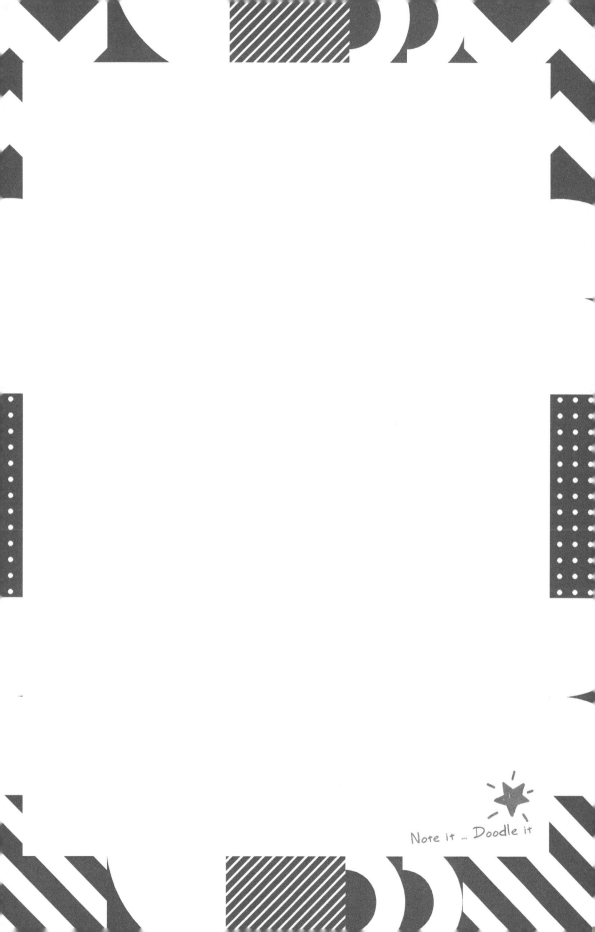

Note it ... Doodle it

Wellbeing Toolkit

Resilience and re-balance

When we are feeling fully on top of our lives, with our relationships flowing well, our workload in a manageable state and plenty to look forward to, challenges can seem well within our capabilities. We are strong and resilient and can easily shoulder the tough times. But when we are overburdened in one or more areas of our lives it is so much harder to find that resilience to keep going. We can more easily break down and may find that we have to take time out for the sake of our physical or mental health.

Resilience is not always a good thing. Being able to withstand an unhealthily tough workload does not take away the fact that the workload needs to be addressed. That said, we can all work on our resilience so that we are in a strong position to speak out when we need help to re-balance our lives. These ideas may support that:

1. Keep an eye on the pattern of your year and anticipate when the extra busy times will be. Plan ahead with healthy freezer meals, back up support from family and friends if possible and maybe a treat or two booked in.

2. If you feel that you are close to being overburdened, ask for help now. Having someone to help you to reprioritise your workload could mean the difference between sinking and swimming.

3. Reframe any negative thinking about taking time out or pulling back on certain aspects of your work or home life. There is no failure in taking control of your wellbeing and actively pursuing a manageable path!

What is on your 'to do' list right now? Choose at least one thing to reprioritise in order to free up space and time for a wellbeing focus so that you can safeguard your resilience. What will you change to free up some time for yourself?

Notes:

··

··

··

··

··

··

··

··

··

Make time for/to: _____

Monday	Tuesday	Wednesday	Thursday	Friday	Saturday	Sunday

MARCH

Highlight/s

....

Notes	Checklist
....	☐
....	☐
....	☐
....	☐

Words are, in my not so humble opinion, our most inexhaustible source of magic.

Dumbledore (J.K.Rowling),

Harry Potter and the Deathly Hallows (2007)

March

- Key dates/Events:

What,
Where,
Who ...

Date

Date

Date

Date

Date

March is the month of World Book Day. This has become a notable date in the calendar for schools, teachers and parents. Whether your school goes all out and asks all the children (and you!) to dress up, or you do something simpler, March is nonetheless a good month to celebrate books and words.

As a primary school teacher, you will be surrounded by books. Your classroom is likely to include a selection of children's fiction and non-fiction books and perhaps children and parents ask you for book recommendations.

In school, reading is often a social activity. Children read together, teachers share stories and books. A school can be a reading community.

Have a think about the books or stories that have shaped the way you feel about reading. Have any inspired you to do something new or to think of something in a different way?

-

-

-

-

-

-

Professional Learning

Communities of readers

Reading can be a genuine joy and pleasure in the lives of those who set aside time to do it. Building communities of readers who are engaged and genuinely enjoy the written word can work wonders for attainment across the curriculum.

In order to build communities of readers in your class, there are some key elements that need to be put in place. Teresa Cremin (2014) explains that teachers need professional knowledge of children's texts and a reading for pleasure pedagogy in their classroom which encompasses:

☐   reading aloud

☐   independent reading time

☐   book talk

A reading teacher is a teacher who reads and a reader who teaches. In communities of readers 'there are strong relationships between teachers and children, and children and children around reading'. Reading can shift from being an individual pursuit to being a social activity.

Broadening your knowledge of children's literature is bound to have a positive impact on reading in your classroom. Teresa Cremin suggests reading books that have won awards such as the Carnegie and Kate Greenaway, Blue Peter, Costa, School Library Association and UK Literary Association. Showcase books you have read and enjoyed and create a library shelf in your classroom and encourage reciprocal recommendations between teachers and children in your school.

Think about the social support children get for reading, the spaces and places that children have to settle down to read, and the opportunities they have to celebrate books and stories in your classroom. Can you make any improvements?

Classroom Ideas

Filling everyone's bucket

One activity that has the huge advantage of being applicable to all primary years, is the bucket filler activity. Based on the book *Have you Filled a Bucket Today?* by Carol McCloud, this activity encourages children to uplift their peers through compliments and kind words.

☐ Use the book as a stimulus, or simply explain the concept.

☐ The bucket represents a person's self-esteem and confidence.

☐ To fill up somebody's bucket requires being kind to others and thinking about what you like about people (this also complements school values and rules).

As a teacher, you could model an example with a student teacher or a TA. Say something nice about that person. Try and keep it specific – 'you did a really great job on that classroom display'. Then give children the opportunity to compliment other people in the class.

This can be a good activity to refer to when children come in hot and bothered from lunch break squabbles, and it impacts the behaviour in the classroom. Emphasise the harm of hurtful words. You might also discuss the impact of saying or doing something mean – 'dipping in' to someone's bucket and removing good thoughts and feelings.

Could you incorporate this into your classroom teaching? When would it be most relevant? Make some notes . . .

Notes:

....

....

....

....

....

....

....

....

....

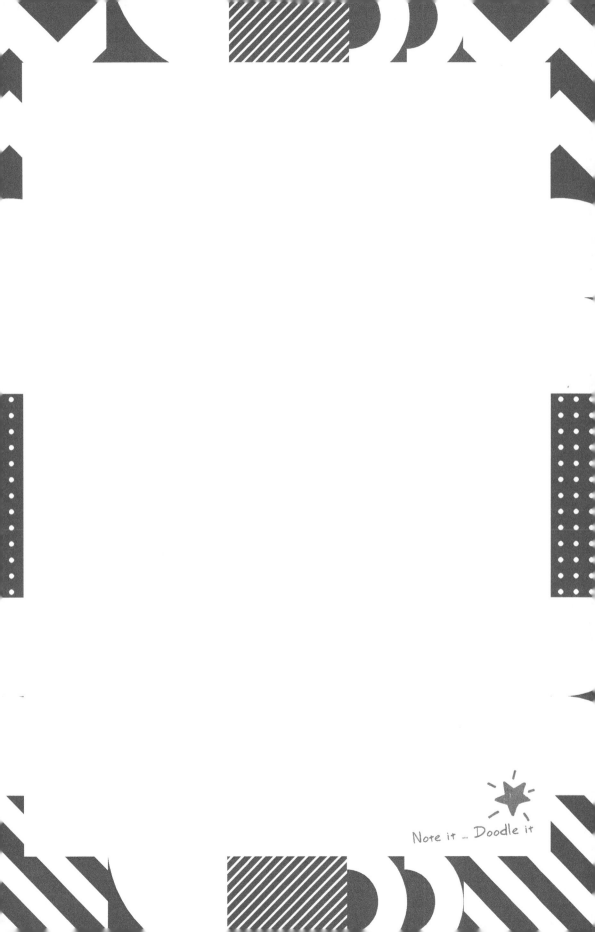

Note it ... Doodle it

Wellbeing Toolkit

Pausing for breath with a book

The chances are you have been working at full capacity since the Christmas break and are in need of some downtime. It is so important to give yourself some escapism that will take you out of your day-to-day demands and enable you to rest and relax. Reading is a brilliant hobby for this purpose, is available free of charge, can be done anytime anywhere and can take you far, far away from your stresses and pressures. It's the perfect de-stressor!

If you're not already reading for pleasure and relaxation, these ideas may help:

1. *Finding time* — Carve out a chunk of time each day for reading. You don't need hours of spare time although you may wish you had it! Just ten minutes a couple of times a day will boost your wellbeing and take you away from your immediate surroundings for a short while.

2. *Book clubs* — Find out if there is a book club in your locality. Your local library will probably have information, or your local facebook pages. You could start a book club with neighbours. There is more information here on getting started https://www.penguinrandomhouse.com/book-clubs/faqs/

3. *Book groups at work* — While reading something for pleasure that is totally unrelated to work is a great thing, you may want to consider setting up a book group within your school to discuss education themes pertinent to your pupils.

BookCrossing is the act of releasing your much-loved books 'into the wild' for a stranger to read next. You can track where they go on the website. Take a look at www.bookcrossing.com to find out more.

Can reading help you find a moment of calm and escape in your working week? How can you make sure you find time for this? Make some notes . . .

Make time for/to: _____

Add the dates for the month

Monday	Tuesday	Wednesday	Thursday	Friday	Saturday	Sunday

APRIL

Highlight/s

....

Notes	Checklist
....	☐
....	☐
....	☐
....	☐

The arts empower children. They contribute to the development of all aspects of a child's potential and personality: studying the arts fosters creativity, innovation, empathy, and resilience. The arts enrich young lives, making them happier and healthier.

Cultural Learning Alliance,
The Arts for Every Child (2019)

April
- Key dates/Events:

What,
Where,
Who ...

Date

Date

Date

Date

Date

Creativity is not something that we can 'add on' to the curriculum. It must be part of the teaching environment and the teaching ethos of all classrooms. Embedding creativity in classroom practice is essential to creating an inclusive, learning friendly space where children are happy and fulfilled (Thorpe, 2019).

Of course 'creativity' is not one thing. Yes, painting can be creative – but not always. It might help to think about creativity in terms of the creative process. Forming an idea, planning, trying things out, making mistakes, keeping going and learning all the time.

How you bring creativity to your classroom will depend on who you are as a teacher and the individual children in your class at any one time. That's OK. Take time to think about what creativity looks like in your classroom this year. How can you bring more creativity to teaching and learning? Make some notes . . .

-

-

-

-

-

-

Professional Learning

Living creatively

If there is one thing that living through the SARS-CoV-2 pandemic taught us, it is that the arts are a crucially important dimension of our wellbeing. Living creatively, growing ourselves through a creative life, can do wonders for our happiness and wellbeing. So it stands to reason that we should give creativity prominence in our teaching of children and young people.

Creativity is not synonymous with art. There are many ways of being creative and of creating. Creativity can, and should, be encouraged right across the curriculum. The Durham Commission on Creativity and Education (https://www.dur.ac.uk/creativitycommission/) sought to explore a creative education and the benefits of creative thinking and practice within these themes: economic growth, skills, and social mobility; community identity and social engagement; and personal fulfilment and wellbeing. You can read up on the findings. Also consider:

1. What cultural activities do your pupils have access to in your school?

2. Are the arts a substantive part of each child's day, or an add on?

3. Have you had any CPD to enhance the provision of arts subjects in your school?

4. How can you improve on the creative curriculum your pupils currently access?

A search on the internet will reveal many books on creativity in schools. You may like to explore the work of Sir Ken Robinson, Debra Kidd and Hywel Roberts for starters.

Consider the questions above. Can your teaching of and focus on creativity in the curriculum be improved? How? Make some notes . . .

Classroom Ideas

Getting creative with maths

Islamic art, as a discipline, uses the principles of geometry to develop intricate patterns. The principles of the golden ratio and how this applies to symmetry are commonly applied to develop intricate geometric patterns. The Alhambra Palace in Granada, Spain has complex geometric patterns, developed by artisans both on tiles as well as stone and wood carvings.

Share some pictures of the geometric patterns from the Alhambra Palace with your class and create your own tessellation art!

☐ Introduce different shapes and get children to examine them.

☐ Which shapes would work best in a repeating/tessellating pattern?

☐ How many of the shapes should we use?

☐ Which different shapes work well together? Why?

☐ What sizes of shapes? How many sides? What kind of angles?

☐ Encourage children to look at the similarities and differences between the shapes, to see patterns.

☐ Use the art resources that work for you and your class. Paint, cut out colourful shapes, fabric, printing/stamps.

Are there other ways for you to bring creative skills to the maths learning in your classroom? Or the science learning? How about history? Take time to brainstorm what might work for you . . .

Notes:

Note it ... Doodle it

Wellbeing Toolkit

Creative wellbeing

Having a creative outlet is an important element of your wellbeing drive. This doesn't need to be professional standard artistry! (Although many teachers have a creative side hustle.) Simply doing something creative that gives you joy and pleasure will support your wellbeing no end.

Research by BBC Arts in partnership with UCL (2019) explored how first-time creative activities can help us boost wellbeing and manage mood. The results showed that there are three main ways we use creativity as coping mechanisms to control our emotions:

1. As a distraction tool — to give ourselves the chance to get away from our day-to-day challenges.

2. As a contemplation tool — to give our minds and bodies the time and space to be calm and reflective.

3. As a means of self-development — to learn new skills.

Trying new creative hobbies is particularly good for us. It doesn't matter how well we do at it, it's the taking part that matters. While recent experiences of lockdowns might have forced us to stay apart from one another, research suggests that the face-to-face social interaction of taking part in live activities is what really boosts our wellbeing.

So, what creative hobby will you take up? There is no end to the potential, and this time of year, with lighter evenings and brighter days, is a great time to pick up something new.

Creativity for Wellbeing (creativity4wellbeing.com) is a free art resource for everyone created by Richard K. Potter. It is packed with ideas that encourage creativity for health and wellbeing. Have a browse and choose an activity to do!

What creative activity helps you? Is there something new that you would like to try? Make some notes . . .

Make time for/to: _____

Add the dates for the month

Monday	Tuesday	Wednesday	Thursday	Friday	Saturday	Sunday

MAY

Highlight/s

....

Notes

....

....

....

....

Checklist

☐

☐

☐

☐

The best classroom and the richest classroom is roofed only by sky.

Margaret McMillan,

Nursery Schools and the Pre-School Child (1925)

May

- Key dates/Events:

What, Where, Who ...

Date

Date

Date

Date

Date

May means Outdoor Classroom Day – 'a global movement to inspire and celebrate outdoor play and learning at home and at school'. For more information, visit: https://outdoorclassroomday. org.uk/about/

There are many benefits to learning and teaching outdoors. The change of learning space and the different stimuli in the outdoor environment can alter the norms of behaviour in a class group. It is sometimes the children that teachers are concerned about taking outside that benefit from it the most. The Council for Learning Outside of the Classroom outlines how this change in environment can have an impact (https://www.lotc.org.uk/why/motivation-and-behaviour/).

Have you found that children's behaviour is different when learning outside? How do you use the outdoor space in your school for learning and teaching? Could you use it more? Make some notes . . .

-
-
-
-
-
-

Professional Learning

The whole curriculum, outdoors

Learning outside is often associated with mud, zip wires, tree climbing, shelter building and fire circles. These things are, of course, important but there is no reason why the whole of the primary curriculum cannot be taken outdoors. If space allows, finding time to think about how to use your school's outdoor space for 'everyday teaching' will help you to embed outdoor learning across the curriculum.

Some ideas for the 'core' subjects:

Doing maths outdoors allows you to use large spaces and is especially useful when teaching about size, measurement and scales. Your playground can be a great physical space for teaching co-ordinates – a huge grid in chalk can allow children to play 'full size' battleships. Learning about volumes of liquids can be made real with bottles of various sizes but the same volume – or different volume but the same height.

Again, the size of the space can be useful for sentence making where children are different words or types of words. Does there need to be a 'verb child' in every sentence? What about SPAG – where in sentences do punctuation marks go? Starting a sentence with a capital letter can have more meaning for some children when they see that a line of children being a 'sentence' has to start with the 'capital letter' child.

There are many ways in which the size of a playground (and the lack of trouble when spilling water!) can support your teaching. For more ideas, download the free guide from the Council for Learning Outside the Classroom: https://www.lotc.org.uk/resources/education-resources/

Classroom Ideas

Computing unplugged: Shoot the Robot

Yes, you can even teach coding outside! In her book *Computing Unplugged*, **Helen Caldwell offers readers a large number of ideas for teaching computing without a computer. This lesson will help children to get a better idea of the commands that are used in programming and the importance of sequencing and precision in coding. It will also help you to get outside and enjoy some May weather!**

1. Small groups of children control one blindfolded human robot with the aim of being the first to get a ball to hit a target or to hit the robot of the opposing team.

2. The robot can only understand a limited number of commands: 'Forward one pace', 'Backward one pace', 'Turn left', 'Turn right' and 'Fire'.

3. Set up a target to be the robot.

Discussion points:

☐ How do we talk to robots and how can they understand what we want them to do?

☐ Can robots play games?

☐ Can we work out a sequence of commands that represents a successful game strategy?

For more details on this lesson and many more lesson ideas, see *Teaching Computing Unplugged in Primary Schools* by Helen Caldwell.

Notes:

Note it ... Doodle it

Wellbeing Toolkit

The gentle art of balance

There is nothing mysterious about wellbeing. What helps us to feel a sense of wellbeing in our lives has been thoroughly researched and is well documented. Perhaps the reason we find it so difficult at times to feel a sense of wellbeing in our lives is that the myriad commitments we juggle get out of balance.

One of the powerful keys to wellbeing is this sense of balance. Without it we risk being overwhelmed by one aspect of our lives or another. It sounds simple, and it is (and don't let anyone tell you otherwise!), but we do have to work at it. If we know that having time to cook a decent meal helps our sense of equilibrium, we need to find time for that. If we find ourselves saying no to every social invitation in order to get on top of work, we need to do something about that. When our lives are in balance, we are better able to stand times of increased pressure, but if we are already out of balance, our chances of being resilient in the face of extra demands are significantly diminished.

Think about how balanced your life feels. Do you have time in your days for work as well as relaxation? What about hobbies and family? Time for retreat and replenishment? This exercise may help:

1. What does balance in your life mean to you?

2. Look at an average week in your term-time life. How is your time divided? How balanced does it feel?

3. What do you currently not give time to that you would like to?

4. What blocks remain in your quest for balance?

Developing a sense of awareness around balance in your life is an ongoing pursuit. It needs your attention on a daily basis. Consider making a note in your diary a few times a week about how balanced your life feels. If more balance is needed, work on it.

Make some notes...

Make time for/ to: _____

Add the dates for the month

Monday	Tuesday	Wednesday	Thursday	Friday	Saturday	Sunday

JUNE

Highlight/s

....

Notes   **Checklist**

....   ☐

....   ☐

....   ☐

....   ☐

Why and how we assess our pupils has an enormous impact on their educational experience and consequently on how and what they learn.

Wynne Harlen,

The Quality of Learning (2007)

June

- Key dates/Events:

What,
Where,
Who ...

Date

Date

Date

Date

Date

Assessment is as much a part of learning as it is teaching. Knowing what you still need to learn is a simple but essential tool. Assessment has different purposes – sometimes to help you to plan exciting lessons, sometimes to 'hold you to account'.

Remember this diversity of purpose when planning for end of year assessments. There will be the inevitable spreadsheet to complete. You will need to make judgements (backed up by 'evidence') of whether children are 'emerging', 'expected' or 'exceeding'. The limitations of assessment are many, varied and much discussed. Remember that summative assessments are only ever a part of the story.

Perhaps the most important 'assessments' are the hundreds of times you 'clock' what a child knows, what they can do and what they need more help with. Ongoing, formative assessment is what teaching is all about. Think about the times in just the last week when you have 'assessed' a child in this way? Take time to be conscious of these. Make a note of them. These are the tools of teaching.

-

-

-

-

-

Professional Learning

The right assessment

Assessment is a core element of your job as a teacher. Assessments are inextricably linked to your work on the curriculum and the decisions you take over how to teach. If you are assessing effectively, your assessments will relate directly to the curriculum and will be part of your toolkit for teaching.

It is important to keep in mind that assessments must have a clear purpose – what do you want them to achieve? There are many assessment tools available to you, so be sure to pick the right one for the job in hand!

The Education Endowment Foundation says that a great assessment has purpose, validity, reliability and value. We need to be sure we are assessing learning, though, and not simply short-term memory.

What assessments do you routinely use in your classroom? How effective do you consider them to be? It's worth discussing this with your line manager or a trusted colleague to help you to determine if any changes need to be made to your assessment practices.

Professor Robert Coe wrote a blog about assessment that encourages teachers to interrogate any assessments they plan to let into their classrooms around certain themes such as construct definition, content validity, freedom from biases and robustness. You can find it here:

http://www.cem.org/blog/would-you-let-this-test-into-your-classroom/

Classroom Ideas

So much more than tests...

We have already discussed how it is important to make use of formative assessments often. This can build your understanding of children's confidence as well as of their progress and attainment.

There are some creative methods to find out how individual children feel about a specific topic/lesson. Some ideas:

☐ Exit cards: children must give you an indication of their confidence in their learning. Give children a selection of emojis to help them articulate their confidence. You may also want to add a question as a formative assessment. Ensure it prompts a written response. It is best presented as a 'compulsory' exercise.

☐ Heads down thumbs up: not only is this a great game, but it can also be used for children to give a 'thumbs up' rating as to how they found a lesson without feeling pressurised by the ratings of peers. 'Heads down' means that children are not influenced by others' responses.

How do you assess children's confidence in their learning in your classroom? How effective is it? How could you do this better to inform your teaching of subsequent lessons? Make some notes . . .

Notes:

....

....

....

....

....

....

....

....

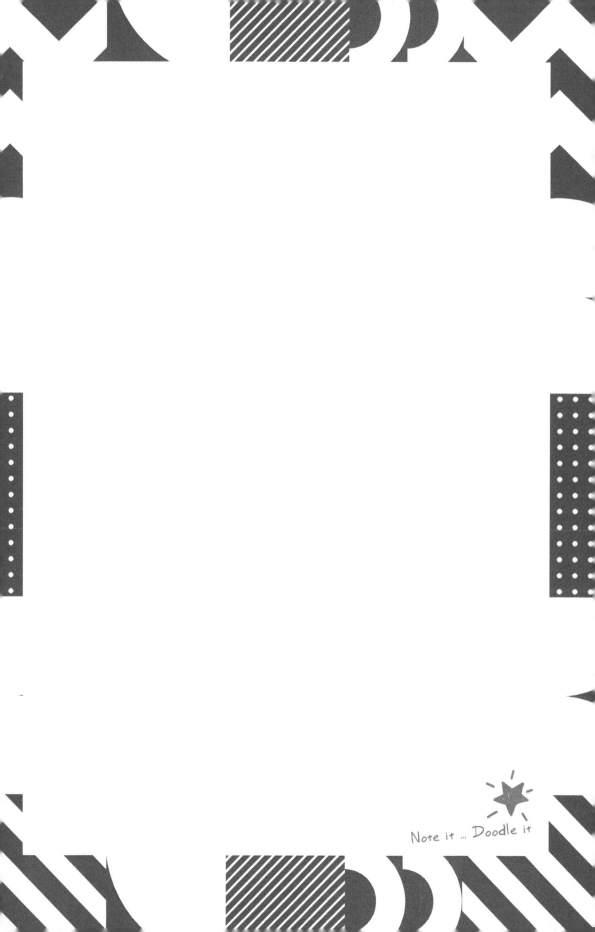

Note it ... Doodle it

Wellbeing Toolkit

Anxiety in focus

If you find that the academic year presents times of heightened anxiety, you may want to focus on ways of recognising and addressing the impact that it has on you. Anxiety can be a perfectly normal response to a perceived threat. But pathological anxiety is more intense and prolonged than day-to-day anxiety and it can be accompanied by other symptoms of mental ill health.

There are many signs that anxiety might be taking hold. You might experience: restlessness, difficulty sleeping, dizziness, difficulty concentrating, irritability, headaches and nausea among other symptoms.

If you experience times of anxiety in your working day, or even panic attacks, mental health charity *Mind* suggests doing the following to ease the symptoms you are feeling:

1. Focus on breathing — breathe slowly in and out to a count of five.

2. Stamp on the spot — this can help you to control your breathing.

3. Focus on your senses — taste a mint-flavoured sweet or touch some soft fabric.

4. Try grounding techniques — listen to the sounds you hear, walk barefoot, touch or sniff something, colour something or write in a journal.

If you find yourself going through repeated periods of high anxiety, you need to address this before your health takes a hit. Your line manager would be a good place to start, and your GP can offer support too.

What strategies work best for you? Have a go at some of those suggested here and use this space to reflect on their usefulness.

Make time for/to: _____

Monday	Tuesday	Wednesday	Thursday	Friday	Saturday	Sunday

JULY

Highlight/s

....

Notes **Checklist**

.... ☐

.... ☐

.... ☐

.... ☐

Surely we have a responsibility to leave for future generations a planet that is healthy and habitable by all species.

Sir David Attenborough,
State of the Planet **(2003)**

July

- Key dates/Events:

What,
Where,
Who ...

Date

Date

Date

Date

Date

Global climate change is happening now. The lives of the children you teach will be impacted by the changes to the planet in ways that we cannot yet imagine. How can primary schools prepare children for such a future?

A good starting place is to make sure you are talking about it. Some studies have shown that children are increasingly anxious about climate change. They see the news, absorb messages and worry about their world. They need to be supported to understand these issues though their education.

Supporting children to better understand the crisis and profiling ways in which people and companies are working to make a difference will have a positive impact. Giving children a sense of agency and showing them how they can make a difference will empower them to be active citizens of the new world they are preparing for.

Consider the resources available to support you to teach about climate change and sustainability and note down which ones you may use.

-

-

-

-

-

Professional Learning

Sustainability for all

Regardless of what the dominant political position may be with regard to climate change, there is an imperative to teach about sustainability across the curriculum. The climate crisis is such that educating for sustainability is now a global priority of the utmost importance.

Organisations such as Learning Through Landscapes and the Geographical Association promote learning outside and offer suggestions for doing so even when you do not have vast school grounds to make use of. You might also like to try these ideas:

1. *Curriculum matters* – Take a good look at your school's curriculum. Audit what happens with regard to the climate and sustainability. The National Association for Environmental Education (NAEE) offers the four Cs as focus points for your audit: curriculum, campus, community, and culture.

2. *Reading and writing* – There are some wonderful young nature writers such as Dara McAnulty and Jessica J. Lee who may inspire your pupils to become more involved in the environment around them.

3. *Sustainable goals* – Explore the seventeen sustainable development goals: https://sdgs.un.org/goals Don't attempt to focus on them all at once, but it is worth picking three or four for your school to explore.

4. *Expert advice* – your local teacher networks may yield some experts who can help to boost enthusiasm and commitment in your school.

5. *Unconscious bias* – watch out for any potential biases in what you teach. It is important to explain when there is more than one way of looking at things.

Good sustainability education is really good education. Harnessing this for the sake of the environment is so important, especially at a time when young people are demanding to learn about sustainability.

Classroom Ideas

Climate Change Dodgeball (from LtL)

Learning Through Landscapes is a UK charity dedicated to enhancing outdoor play and learning. Their website includes free resources and lesson ideas to help you take learning outside. www.ltl.org.uk

This active game from LtL scaffolds pupils' scientific understanding of the greenhouse effect and global warming.

1. Divide the pupils into 2 groups, twice as many in the centre of the circle as those forming a circle around them.

2. The pupils in the centre are Earth. Those on the outside are greenhouse gases (GG).

3. One individual is the Sun outside the atmosphere who throws 'rays' in the form of bean bags at the Earth.

4. The Earth pupils repel the bean bags by throwing them back out of the circle. This represents the heat being reflected from the Earth's surface.

5. The GG pupils try to catch or block the bean bags from leaving the circle and throw them back at the Earth.

6. The round ends when all the bean bags are outside the circle. Since most of the children are in the centre it should end quickly.

7. In subsequent rounds, increase the number of GG pupils, explaining that there are more in the atmosphere due to human actions. It is then harder for the heat to escape the Earth's atmosphere.

8. At the end, you can put one brave pupil in the centre for dramatic effect.

For more detailed instructions on the activity and for discussion points, see: https://www.ltl.org.uk/resources/climate_change_dodgeball/

Notes:

....

....

....

....

....

....

....

....

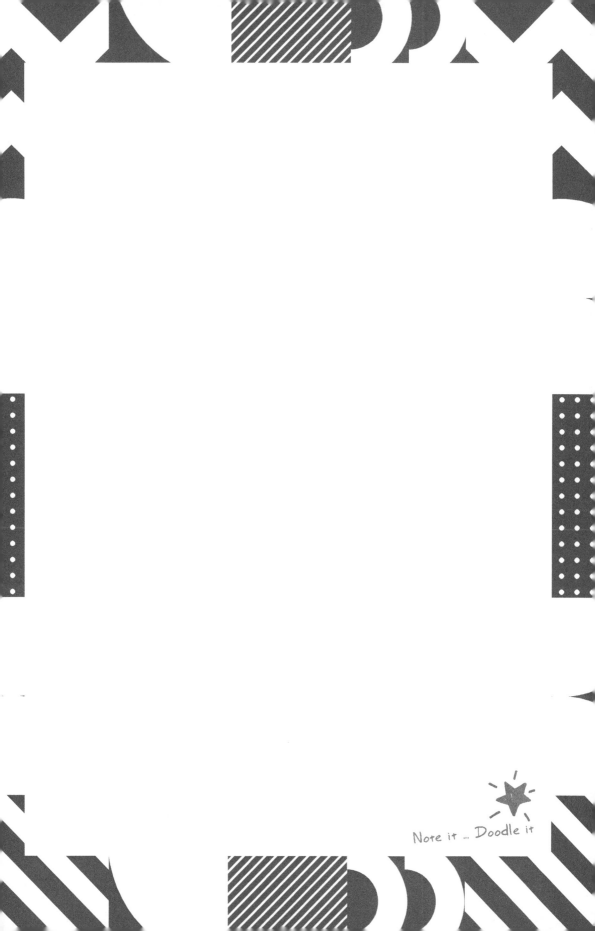

Note it ... Doodle it

Wellbeing Toolkit

Wellbeing matters

It's July, and you may well be feeling a blend of excitement, exhaustion and overwhelm at completing an academic year. That's perfectly normal! But at times, the feelings we have about the impact that our work is having on us could do with a little external support to help get us back on an even keel.

Asking for help is one of the most self-nurturing things we can do. There is a tendency to put it off while we try to cope stoically, possibly blocking out our feelings of carrying too much, but this ultimately leads to imbalance and difficulties further down the road.

If this academic year has been at all challenging or even traumatic, please know that help is out there for you. There are many potential sources, so don't ever feel that you must struggle on alone:

☐ Your line manager or another trusted colleague may be able to help you to gain some perspective on your specific circumstances. They may also be able to help you to reprioritise your work to free up space for wellbeing purposes. This can be particularly helpful if you are anticipating a stressful academic year ahead.

☐ Your GP will be able to signpost appropriate sources of support for you, as well as doing some basic health checks such as blood pressure and a full blood count.

☐ Your union's website will carry wellbeing support and may also have specific support for any issues you are facing at school. They may have a confidential helpline too which could prove to be supportive.

☐ Education Support Partnership offers mental health and wellbeing support for education professionals in schools, colleges and universities. It runs a helpline that you can access 24/7. You

can call on 08000 562561 or visit the website
www.educationsupport.org.uk

☐ Life Squared offers an immense amount of high-quality
wellbeing support free of charge on its website:
www.lifesquared.org.uk

It is really important to address any wellbeing concerns you have now rather than shelving them until after the summer holidays. That way you can have a genuine break and look to the term ahead with confidence.

Make some notes about your wellbeing concerns in the space below.

Make time for/ to: _____

Monday	Tuesday	Wednesday	Thursday	Friday	Saturday	Sunday

AUGUST

Highlight/s

....

Notes

....

....

....

....

Checklist

☐

☐

☐

☐

I may not have gone where I intended to go, but I think I have ended up where I needed to be.

Douglas Adams,

The Long Dark Tea-Time of the Soul (1988)

August
- Key dates/Events:

What,
Where,
Who ...

Date

Date

Date

Date

Date

In a work time planner for primary school teachers it may seem strange to have an entry for August. This is a month of rest and perhaps some planning for what comes next. What professional learning is there in that? What support for my wellbeing do I need if I am not working? The answer to both of these questions is 'lots'.

Taking time to simply reflect on the year you have had and take stock has huge value to you as a professional. With some space and time, you will be able to consider what worked well for you and what you would like do better, or transform, for next term. Don't underestimate the value of this. Even if you write nothing down to record this thinking, it is happening, and you are learning.

Times of rest are not always stress free. It can be that the busyness of term time is masking some issues that you have not yet worked through. These can come to the surface when day to day stress eases. Some can find holidays difficult.

This month we have provided some space. Space to list the things you have learned from last year and to consider what your development needs might be for the future. You might also like to make some resolutions for the year ahead.

We also provide you with some tips to support you to get the most out of any rest time you have.

-

-

-

Notes:

....

....

....

....

....

....

....

....

Notes:

Note it ... Doodle it

Wellbeing Toolkit

Retreat, replenish, restore

At the end of a long, and hopefully fulfilling and enriching academic year, it is so important to restore your sense of balance and replenish your energy. You cannot plough on through your holiday at the same pace and level of productivity that you do through the term times. There is a real risk of burnout if you try!

Aim to create some pockets of time in which you plan for the academic year ahead, but be sure to limit this time so that it doesn't bleed into other aspects of your life. Prepare a realistic list of what you want to achieve and don't be tempted to add to it. This way, any work you do during the holiday will be contained and should not adversely affect your wellbeing. It is also worth remembering that feeling ready and prepared for the year ahead can actually contribute positively to your wellbeing.

The main focus of your holiday, however, must be relaxation, restoration and replenishment so that you are emotionally and physically ready for the academic year ahead. These ideas may help:

1.   Spotlight on food — think about your diet during term time. If you have slipped into some habits that may not be the healthiest, now is the time to fix that. Focusing on increasing your intake of fruits and vegetables and limiting food containing excessive amounts of fat and sugar can be a great place to start. Keeping your fluid intake up is wise too.

2.   Retreating and replenishing — retreats can be deeply fulfilling and restoring. They do not need to have a religious element to them and it is not even necessary to leave your home. The key is to set your mind to withdrawing from what causes you stress and anxiety and give yourself a mental break from it. Do whatever does it for you — long baths, a run, some walks, reading a nourishing book… there are many possibilities for deep rest.

Think about the year ahead and the pace and rhythm of your weeks. When can you retreat once the term is in full flow? Aim to protect some mid-week evenings and weekends so that you can experience some deep relaxation even in the midst of a busy term.

Make time for/to: _____

References

September

Thompson, C. and Wolstencroft, P. (2021) *The Trainee Teacher's Handbook* (2nd edition). London: SAGE Publications.

Yousafzai, M. and Lamb, C. (2014) *I Am Malala*. London: Weidenfeld & Nicolson.

October

Bottrill, G. (2020) *School and the Magic of Children*. London: SAGE Publications.

OECD (2020) https://www.oecd-ilibrary.org/docserver/f8d7880d-en.pdf?expires=1614180157&id=id&accname=guest&checksum=44878296A723E872D5D871D7203527AB).

November

Education Endowment Foundation (EEF) (2018) https://educationendowmentfoundation.org.uk/tools/guidance-reports/working-with-parents-to-support-childrens-learning/

Washington, B.T. (1969 [1900]) *Story of My Life and Work*. New York: Negro Universities Press.

December

Centre for Literacy in Primary Education (CLPE) (2018) https://clpe.org.uk/blog/2018/why-drama-essential-todays-classrooms

Owens, J. and Neimark, P. (1970) *Blackthink: My Life as Black Man and White Man*. New York: William Morrow and Company, Inc.

January

Obama, M. (2017) Speech to honour the '2017 School Counselor of the Year' in the East Room of the White House, January 2017.

February

Castle, P. and Buckler, S. (2021) *Psychology for Teachers* (2nd edition). London: SAGE Publications.

March

Cremin, T., Mottram, M., Powell, S., Collins, R. and Safford, K. (2014) *Building Communities of Engaged Readers: Reading for pleasure*. London and NY: Routledge.

McCloud, C. (2015) *Have You Filled a Bucket Today?* Brighton: Bucket Fillers.

Rowling, J.K. (2007) *Harry Potter and the Deathly Hallows*. London: Bloomsbury.

April

BBC Arts and UCL (2019) https://www.bbc.co.uk/mediacentre/latestnews/2019/get-creative-research

Cultural Learning Alliance *The Arts for Every Child* (2019) Arts-for-every-child-CLA-Social-justice-briefing.pdf (culturallearningalliance.org.uk)

Thorpe, K. (2019) 'Chapter 1: *Resourcing the Spirit of the Child: Creativity in the Contemporary Classroom*' in *A Broad and Balanced Curriculum in Primary Schools*, edited by Ogier, S. London: SAGE Publications.

May

Caldwell, H. (2016) *Teaching Computing Unplugged in Primary Schools*. London: SAGE Publications.

McMillan, M. (1925) *Nursery Schools and the Pre-school Child* (pamphlet). London: Nursery School Association.

June

Harlen, W. (2007) *The Quality of Learning: Assessment Alternatives for Primary Education*, Primary Review Research Survey 3/4. Cambridge: University of Cambridge Faculty of Education. https://cprtrust.org.uk/wp-content/uploads/2014/06/research-survey-3-4.pdf

July

Attenborough, Sir D. (2003) "State of the Planet with David Attenborough", first broadcast BBC One November 2003.

August

Adams, D. (1988) *The Long Dark Tea-Time of the Soul*. Hampshire: Heinemann.

a little guide for teachers

THIS SERIES IS LITTLE IN SIZE BUT BIG ON ALL THE SUPPORT AND INSPIRATION YOU NEED TO NAVIGATE YOUR DAY-TO-DAY LIFE AS A TEACHER.

Books in the series include:

Find out more at:

www.sagepub.co.uk/littleguides